GODFULNESS

"The ceaseless pace and activity of the modern world takes a heavy toll on any relationship with God. Bible reading in particular has become something that is done poorly, if at all. We slot our time with God's Word into spare moments and, reading the text with speed, fail to feed on it properly. It's hardly surprising that spiritual malnourishment has reached epidemic proportions.

This invaluable little book from Derek Leaf addresses with wisdom, grace and experience how we can best interact with the Bible. He makes a compelling call for to us to pause, read the Word carefully, and let it soak deep down in enriching and renewing power into our lives.

A good book blesses you but a great book teaches you how to be blessed. This is one of those."

REVD CANON J.JOHN

GODFULNESS
A Step-by-step Guide to Bible Meditation
BY DEREK LEAF

Navigators UK

Copyright © 2017 Derek Leaf. All rights reserved.

First paperback edition printed 2017 in the United Kingdom

A catalogue record for this book is available from the British Library

ISBN 978-1-900964-27-2

Published by Navigators UK (www.navigators.co.uk)

Printed by Stanbury Chameleon

www.sc-print.co.uk

Printed in Great Britain

CONTENTS

PREFACE

For years I have pondered the meaning of life. Then, while praying Paul's prayers for others, I realised the answer was right in front of me, there in those prayers. Paul had learnt what God values as important in life. This then transformed the way he lived and what he desired to see in the lives of others. How did I discover this? Through meditating on these words from the Bible, through focusing my heart and mind on what was written, through spending unrushed time praying about its meaning.

My hope is that in this book you will learn how to meditate on the Bible and find out what is important to God. As we discover his values, they can affect our choices, and God can empower us in every aspect of our lives. Through these insights our lives can change and we can begin to work with God on things that have eternal significance.

God wants us to grow in our understanding of him, and he wants us to share it with others. The things we think about, pray about and meditate on will guide our conversations. Meditating on Paul's prayers can become a launching pad from which we can venture out with God. His strategic approach enables us to understand how to pray and how to help others grow in God.

Since the essence of life is a relationship with God, the meaning of life is not a series of instructions to be lived out independently of him, but a dynamic process that we are led through by him. Part of that process is learning to hear from God through Bible meditation. This book aims to help you understand what God would have you live for. The Bible says, *"Help me understand the meaning of your commandments, and I will meditate on your wonderful deeds"* (Psalm 119:27).

Spend time reflecting on each of Paul's prayers. They will guide you and those you help. They will change your life.

God bless,

Derek Leaf

Where to Start:
INTRODUCING GODFULNESS

Godfulness is a hands-on guide to meditating on the Bible. You'll learn Bible meditation by doing it. Set aside some time alone to get stuck in. Read a chapter at a time, allowing space between sittings in order to ponder, pray over and apply the Bible verses in your everyday life. Each chapter guides you through a meditation on a Bible passage, with questions to help you engage. Along the way, you'll experience a variety of different techniques, heart issues and effects of Bible meditation.

The passages chosen are the Apostle Paul's prayers, making these meditations an exploration of life's purpose. To help you, I have added some thoughts from my personal meditation on these passages, and stories of their impact on my life. By meditating your way through Paul's prayers, you will discover, and come to own, the tools you need to meditate on any part of Scripture.

How Paul looked at life

Sometimes we want to celebrate life. Other times life can be very hard. We may wonder if there is a meaning or purpose to life. We may wonder if there is a certain way we should live.

These are matters the Bible explores, and its truths can change our lives. We will look at what Paul prayed for the many churches he started. What he discovered as he encountered God is just as relevant today.

What gives meaning to your life?

Many want success and happiness out of life. Many want God to fulfil their dreams. They want him to do exactly what they demand. But often God doesn't seem to comply, and people get frustrated. This very frustration raises the question: what are God's purposes for us?

Paul tells us. *"There is one God, the Father, by whom all things were created, and for whom we live. And there is one Lord, Jesus Christ, through whom all things were created, and through whom we live"* (1 Corinthians 8:6). God made us to live for him. He made us to live through Jesus, our only Lord.

This answer is challenging. We may be living for other things. Our life's pursuits are called into question.

Paul knew where to go when faced with difficult questions. He said, *"When I think of all this, I fall to my knees and pray to the Father"* (Ephesians 3:14). As he thought about God he prayed to God. He knew that through prayerfully meditating on God he would be shown the way. We can do the very same thing and it begins with a hunger for God.

> - What things about God and life confuse you?

> - How could you approach God about these?

It starts with prayer

We want to live our lives for God, but how do we do this practically? Paul gives us a clue in his prayer for his friends. *"We ask God… [that] the way you live will always honor and please the Lord"* (Colossians 1:9-10). Take a few minutes to pray about these verses from Colossians. Ask God to open your heart and mind. Ask him to show you what it means and how it can apply to your life. Without God, we cannot truly give our lives to God, we cannot truly bring him honour and joy.

- What do you think God would like to see in your life?

- How do you think you could give your life to God?

Now look at another verse. Paul wrote, *"I pray that… Christ will make his home in your hearts as you trust in him"* (Ephesians 3:16-17). Pray about this verse as well. Again, ask God to show you his heart. Ask him what this verse could mean for you. God wants to hold nothing back. He gave his son, Jesus, to live with you and become integral to your life.

- How do you think Jesus can make his home in you?

- What does it feel like to know that Jesus wants you to be his home?

Did you notice that the giving is two way? We give ourselves to God, and God gives of himself to us. Paul says we will be *"made complete with all the fullness of life and power that comes from God"* (Ephesians 3:19). We will be *"filled with joy, always thanking the Father"* (Colossians 1:11-12). We will be *"filled with the fruit of … salvation – the righteous character produced in [our lives] by Jesus Christ"* (Philippians 1:11).

- This is a lot to take in. Spend the next week thinking on these verses. Write them out on cards. Carry them with you.

- Pray about them, that they would begin to impact your life.

Meditating on God's Word becomes a divine partnership! He shows you his heart and then, as you pray about and begin to act on what he has shown you, your heart is changed.

My prayer is that this journey leads you into a deeper relationship with God and a richer understanding of his purposes for your life.

A Dynamic Partnership:
BIBLE MEDITATION IS BASED ON TRUST

Have you had times when you didn't understand why something was happening?

> - Reflect on these times.

> - How were your emotions affected? Did you respond well?

> - Could it have been an opportunity to see what God was doing?

Start with prayer, asking God to guide you. Now read through the following verses a number of times. If you are able, read them in several different translations.

> *I pray that your love will overflow more and more, and that you will keep on growing in knowledge and understanding. For I want you to understand what really matters, so that you may live pure and blameless lives until the day of Christ's return. May you always be filled with the fruit of your salvation – the righteous character produced in your life by Jesus Christ – for this will bring much glory and praise to God.* (Philippians 1:9-11)

- What is the reason for this passage?

- How do you think knowledge and understanding could affect your love?

- What would it look like to have your character changed by Jesus?

Keep meditating on this passage. You are not looking for a 'right answer' but are looking for thoughts that speak to your heart. If you notice, Paul asked God to develop these people into vibrant Christians. He believed that they could trust God enough to let him work in them. This is a dynamic partnership.

Let's go even deeper.

- *"I pray that your love will overflow more and more..."* How can God give you the inner resources to love beyond your natural capability?

- *"...and that you will keep on growing in knowledge and understanding."* How can understanding God shape the way you live?

- *"For I want you to understand what really matters..."* How does a perspective on what is important in life help you overflow in love?

- *"...so that you may live pure and blameless lives..."* What choices do you think would be involved in living a godly life?

- *"...filled with the fruit of your salvation – the righteous character produced in your life by Jesus Christ..."* How have you seen Jesus develop your character as you have partnered with him?

It all comes down to trust. Meditating on God's Word helps us to develop life-changing trust. Here is a story from my life…

I was working to a deadline on a project, but getting nowhere. As I worked, my two-year-old son appeared with a book he wanted me to read. Every part of me screamed, Noooo! I didn't have time; I was feeling the pressure. Yet, could I trust God to get me through? I knew the maths: there wasn't enough time to entertain a child and do my work. But God had shown me his love again and again. Could I not extend it to my son? I stopped what I was doing and read to him. Yet I prayed for God to rescue me. But my son asked me to read his story again and again. I could barely contain my frustration and show him love… Despite that setback, my project was well received. God answered my prayer as I trusted in him.

- Have you ever seen God at work in your life?

- Think over the verses we looked at earlier (Philippians 1:9-11). What feelings do they draw from your heart?

- What would it mean for you to love people as God loves you?

Trust is developed through meditating on God's Word. It becomes a partnership between God and you.

A Faith-stretching Challenge:
BIBLE MEDITATION TAKES PERSISTENCE

Take a few minutes to think of a time when you were pushed outside of your comfort zone.

    - How did you react?

    - Did you think to bring God into your situation?

Read the following verses several times. Pray that God would fill you with understanding. Then think of how God has been faithful to you in the past. It will encourage you as you learn to trust him for new things.

> We always thank God for all of you and pray for you constantly. As we pray to our God and Father about you, we think of your faithful work, your loving deeds, and the enduring hope you have because of our Lord Jesus Christ. (1 Thessalonians 1:2-3)

Think about these questions as you meditate on the passage.

    - Who is Paul giving thanks for?

- What are the things for which he gives thanks?

- Why are these areas of life so important?

- How is God involved in each of these areas?

These are some thoughts that I had... This dynamic partnership between God and us takes us beyond our natural limitations. God works through us and it changes us, but it also affects those around us. Paul recognised this. He said, "*We always thank God for all of you and pray for you...*". He rejoiced in what God was doing in his people.

- *"faithful work"* – God's strength will take us to the end.

- *"loving deeds"* – God's steadfast love overflows from us to others.

- *"enduring hope"* – Jesus' intervention encourages us to persevere.

This has been true in my life...

> A homeless man was selling the *Big Issue* magazine at a train station entrance. He made eye contact, wanting me to buy one. But I didn't have enough money for him and me. When I reached the end of my trip, I still needed to get a bus home or face a long walk, and it had been a long day. I lowered my head and walked past him.
>
> God, however, has a way of not letting us get away with things. I realised that I was putting my hope in bus money instead of God. The only way to return to a right place with God was to accept his challenge in faith. I stopped, walked back and gave the homeless man all my change. We had a brief chat, but it turned out the money was not enough for a magazine, so I said he could just keep it. He was happy, not just with the money, but with some human interaction.

As the train drew into my station I stood up to go. I took one final look around me to check whether I had left anything behind. There on my seat was a pound coin, enough for my bus fare!

What about you? Think about the verses we looked at earlier (1 Thessalonians 1:2-3).

- Have you ever seen God work through you to produce something better than you could have worked out yourself?

- How did it make you feel about God? How did it affect your relationship with him?

- To develop faithfulness, love and hope, it takes persistence. How could you develop your relationship with God to the point where you could trust him to cover you when you take such risks?

Don't give up on meditating on the Bible. Instead, rise to the challenge. Go buy a diary or journal. Write down what you are learning, and keep a record of what God is doing. God is working in your life.

Abundant Growth:
BIBLE MEDITATION REQUIRES LETTING GO

Has there been a time in your life when you felt like everything was going well in your relationships, your work, your rest?

- Stop and reflect on one good situation.

- What do you think contributed to your feelings of wellbeing?

- Did you do anything to maintain it?

Spend some time reading through this passage from Colossians 1. Pray about it, asking God to open your heart and your mind. Read it several more times, and this time write down your observations.

> *So we have not stopped praying for you since we first heard about you. We ask God to give you complete knowledge of his will and to give you spiritual wisdom and understanding. Then the way you live will always honor and please the Lord, and your lives will produce every kind of good fruit. All the while, you will grow as you learn to know God better and better.* (Colossians 1:9-10)

Let's dig a bit deeper.

- Pick out the specific things Paul prays for the Colossians.

- What do you think of each of the things Paul prays for? How would you
  feel if these attributes began influencing your choices?

- What is the outcome that Paul desires when his prayers are answered?
  Could that be your desire?

Bible meditation is more than just a hobby. It can be a life-changing exercise.
Here are some thoughts I had as I meditated on this passage – observations and
questions that profoundly changed my life.

- Paul put into practice what he believed. He said, *"…we have not
  stopped praying for you since we first heard about you."* Could we live
  our lives with such dedication?

- He was specific. *"We ask God to give you complete knowledge of his
  will and to give you spiritual wisdom and understanding."* Do we dare
  to receive this gift from God? Could we let go of our will in order to
  receive his?

- He knew how people should live. *"Then the way you live will always
  honor and please the Lord…"* Do we desire God enough to realign our
  lives?

- He prayed for his friends to flourish. *"…your lives will produce every
  kind of good fruit."* It sounds like hard work. Can we knuckle down
  and get going?

- He prayed that they would spend time with God. *"…you will grow as you learn to know God better and better."* This was the key. Can we give up our agenda to develop a relationship with God?

This is one way in which I grappled with letting go of my agenda and putting God first…

> At university, I was encouraged to make a commitment to God concerning my spiritual input. I was not very consistent, but I tried. Later, I prayed that God would help me become disciplined. Then, for years, I could not go to sleep until I had completed three disciplines: read three Bible chapters; pray and reflect on a Bible passage; and review memorised Bible verses. Sometimes I would lie awake for hours trying to sleep until, in a fit of irritation, I would finish the neglected discipline, go back to bed and be asleep as my head hit the pillow.

> Many years later, my wife, who knows me best, asked me a question: "Derek! I don't know what it is, but you have been struggling this week. Is there something spiritual you normally do that you haven't bothered doing?"

> I thought about it. It was reviewing Bible verses. I restarted immediately.

God wants us to flourish in him. Meditating on his Word will help us do this.

- Can you set aside time each day to spend in God's Word? Could it become as consistent as eating, drinking and sleeping? Make a choice. Ask God to help you.

- Ask a Christian who you respect if they could share with you how they receive from God.

An Empowered Life:
BIBLE MEDITATION WILL CHANGE US

We all must make choices in life.

- Stop and reflect on some choices you have recently made.

- Are there things you do because you want to bring honour to God?

- Have these choices significantly changed your life? How?

As you prepare for the next step in Bible meditation, consider the sentence "I did not eat your cake". Have a look at what happens to the meaning when you emphasise a different word in each reading.

- "I **did not** eat your cake."

- "I did not **eat** your cake."

- "I did not eat **your** cake."

- "I did not eat your **cake**."

The sense of the sentence changes completely. Now, take time to pray, and then read the passage below several times. With each reading, put the emphasis on a different set of words. What new insights develop with each reading?

So we keep on praying for you, asking our God to enable you to live a life worthy of his call. May he give you the power to accomplish all the good things your faith prompts you to do. Then the name of our Lord Jesus will be honored because of the way you live, and you will be honored along with him. This is all made possible because of the grace of our God and Lord, Jesus Christ. (2 Thessalonians 1:11-12)

Just as an emphasis on different words could change the meaning of a sentence, so also a change of emphasis in our lives can change the meaning of our lives. These questions will help you as you continue in your meditations.

- What does Paul pray for the Thessalonians? Can we accept these things for ourselves as well?

- What does it mean for our faith to prompt us into action? How can we live for God?

- What is the desired outcome of these prayers? Can we embrace these outcomes as our own?

When meditating on the Bible it is often helpful to look up the meaning of words. For example, "to honour" means to acknowledge the value of someone or something and act accordingly. When we prize Jesus enough to obey him, our lives demonstrate his worth. Shockingly, the word "honoured" is also attributed to us, even though we are only able to live for him through his power and grace.

There are other words you might like to look up as well. You can use a dictionary, a Bible dictionary, or a website such as biblehub.com. There are many good resources out there, resources that will help you meditate on Scripture, and help you change.

Change is a challenge for many of us. I came upon a vivid example one day…

A double-glazing salesman knocked on our door. It was obvious he liked money, and he had all its trappings: nice car, expensive watch, silk suit. After measuring up our front door, he asked about my line of work. "Christian ministry," I said.

He wanted to know about our way of life and how we were paid. When I explained that we were not paid but looked to God to provide for us, he was shocked. But there was something about our values that spoke to his heart. We talked for two intense hours. Finally, he said that he really wanted what we had, and he could see the difference it made, but he wasn't sure if he wanted to let go of his extravagant lifestyle. Like the rich young ruler, he went away sad. He couldn't even bring himself to give us a quote for the door.

This man had seen in our family a life worthy of God's call. It wasn't something we were trying to project. We had no pretences, yet it was enough to be a catalyst. God could do business with that salesman. What about you?

- Re-read the verses from 2 Thessalonians. Pray about them. Is God doing business with you?

- Think about the verses. Is there a certain emphasis that speaks to your heart?

- Is there a key word or thought that could become a part of your life? Let God change you. Let him give you the power.

Extreme Love:
BIBLE MEDITATION AFFECTS OTHERS

All of us know that we do not stand as isolated individuals in this world. All of us have some kind of influence, even though we might not be aware of it.

- Consider a time when you faced a difficulty. How did it affect those around you?

- Reflect on a wonderful episode in your life. How did people react?

Now imagine you find yourself in a great stadium packed with people watching you play the game of life. Read the following verses. Then, imagine Paul as the commentator, describing you. He calls you strong, blameless and holy. What difference would it make to the way you live? How would it affect those with you on the field of play?

> And may the Lord make your love for one another and for all people grow and overflow, just as our love for you overflows. May he, as a result, make your hearts strong, blameless, and holy as you stand before God our Father when our Lord Jesus comes again with all his holy people. Amen. (1 Thessalonians 3:12-13)

Take some time to pray as you read these verses again and again.

- What does it mean for love to overflow?

- Why does God make us strong, blameless and holy?

- Why is it important to be able to stand before God when Jesus comes again?

Jesus often spoke out about a partnership of caring for each other. He said, *"Love each other. Just as I have loved you, you should love each other"* (John 13:34). Paul prayed the same for his friends. Let's dig a bit deeper and explore the plans God has for us. These plans will affect those with whom we rub shoulders.

- God's abundant love: *"…may the Lord make your love for one another and for all people grow and overflow"*. How could God's love in you affect those around you?

- God's strengthening love: *"May he… make your hearts strong, blameless, and holy as you stand before God"*. How would you recognise a strong or holy heart?

- God's rewarding love: *"…as you stand before God our Father when our Lord Jesus comes again with all his holy people."* How does this make us feel about ourselves?

Meditating on what Jesus would like to do in our lives, and then working with him to bring it into being, will profoundly affect us and those around us. I have experienced this in my life…

I was a bit shocked that, when meditating on a verse, I felt Jesus was asking me to go after lost sheep. What was he thinking? As I understood it, my ministry was to raise up leaders for ministry. Little did I realise the work that needed to be done in my own heart, let alone in others.

14

At that time I led a Bible study with a group who only sometimes showed up. I was frustrated and told God I wanted to give up. Whenever people stop coming to a Bible study group I lead, I fill in the blanks. I assume that I have probably caused offence and I can't cope with the thought of facing their rejection. Through meditating on several verses God showed me that he died for these students as well, and I should show them some of that same love. I began to visit them. The first of these lost sheep was delighted to see me. He had been struggling under the pressure of exams and my caring encouraged him. What an encouragement from God to me. And through these visits I discovered that one of the group was probably not a believer. Over the year he gradually began to express a measure of faith in God.

What about you? Re-read the verses from 1 Thessalonians.

- How has Jesus shown you his generous love?

- Who are the people around you that you find challenging to love?

- Pray specifically for these people, asking God to open the way for you to show them practical love.

Overflowing Hope:
BIBLE MEDITATION GIVES CONFIDENCE

All of us have things we worry about. They consume our time, emotions and energy.

> - Why do you think there are times when we are weighed down by anxiety?

> - In such times, what is it that keeps us from being joyful or at peace?

Take some time to read through this passage from Romans 15. Pray about it, emphasise different words, look up a few definitions. Then think on the verse again, and focus on one word: "source". Let your imagination play around with the various uses of this word – it could be a journalist's contact, the start of a river, an academic reference. Where does your imagination go?

Now add into this the idea that God is the source, and that he is the source of hope. Where does this linking of thoughts take you?

> *I pray that God, the source of hope, will fill you completely with joy and peace because you trust in him. Then you will overflow with confident*

hope through the power of the Holy Spirit. (Romans 15:13)

Let's continue with some more linked-up thinking as you meditate on this verse.

- What links hope with joy and peace?

- What would happen if other things were our source of hope?

- What do you think it would look like for you to overflow with confident hope?

God gave Paul the hope he needed when his life was a mess, and Paul prays for this same hope for all those who read his letter. He wants to connect us to the source that helped him through life. He prays for us to receive the same incredible benefits…

- Hope: *"I pray that God, the source of hope…"* What is hope? Is it possible to trust that God will intervene?

- Completeness: *"…will fill you completely with joy and peace…"* Is it possible to be filled with joy and peace, despite our circumstances? How?

- Trust: *"…because you trust in him."* What is the basis of hope?

- Confidence: *"Then you will overflow with confident hope…"* If hope is contagious, how can it overflow from our lives into the lives of others?

- Help: *"…through the power of the Holy Spirit."* We can do nothing on our own. How does it make you feel to know that such a generous God has linked us to himself?

Hope is an unusual thing. It goes against the facts. I experienced it first-hand…

I was in a traffic jam. I was going to miss my plane! I sat there racked by anxiety. The whole company was being rewarded for years of hard work with a weekend trip. I would be humiliated by my obvious absence.

I suddenly realised that I had never even prayed about taking this trip. Everyone was going and I just said yes. I realised that I needed to surrender the trip to God. If he didn't want me there, then so be it. I had recently been doing some Bible study and meditating on Philippians 4, which talks of replacing anxiety with thanks. To give thanks now seemed ridiculous, but I decided to do it anyway. As I let go of my determination to be at the airport, a wave of peace rolled over me. This was not just a restoration of enough equilibrium to survive, this was going from –10 to +10 in a moment. It was going from no hope to hope that God would do good things, even if one of them was for me to miss the plane.

After I had come down off the high of hope, the cars began to move and I made it to the airport for a very enjoyable trip.

Spend some more time meditating on the verse from Romans 15. Link it to a situation in your life.

- When anxiety strikes, what is your immediate 'go to' place for a solution? Is it money? Your clever ideas? Avoidance? Certain people? Influence? ...

- Such 'go to' places are a pointer to where we actually put our hope. What would be involved in letting go of these places?

- Ask God to help you grow in him, for him to become your source of confident hope.

God-centered Wisdom:
BIBLE MEDITATION IMPARTS UNDERSTANDING

There are moments when light dawns as you suddenly understand something that has eluded you. It could be how to complete an important task, why someone had behaved in a strange way...

- Think of a time when you had loads of questions. How did you find answers?

- How would you feel if you never found the answers?

I was walking in the countryside with my wife one day. We came across some people looking out at a mansion across the valley. They asked if it belonged to us! Imagine if this was actually true for you – if you were the heir to a stately home, how would you gain the understanding necessary to take care of your inheritance? In this passage from Ephesians 1, it says that we are God's inheritance. What does that mean? Spend a minute praying before you read it. Ask God to give you wisdom and understanding. Then think about what being an inheritance might mean. Now read the passage through. How does the time spent thinking about it beforehand influence your understanding now?

I have not stopped thanking God for you. I pray for you constantly, asking God, the glorious Father of our Lord Jesus Christ, to give you spiritual wisdom and insight so that you might grow in your knowledge of God. I pray that your hearts will be flooded with light so that you can understand the confident hope he has given to those he called – his holy people who are his rich and glorious inheritance. (Ephesians 1:16-18)

- What are the implications for your life that you are God's inheritance?

- It might be hard to imagine that we are considered rich and glorious. How does that make you feel?

One of Paul's goals was to help people understand who they are in God, and to trust him enough to receive from him. Let's take this prayer and meditate on it phrase by phrase.

- *"I pray for you constantly, asking God... to give you spiritual wisdom and insight..."* Why do you think spiritual wisdom can only come from God? What does that imply?

- *"...so that you might grow in your knowledge of God."* Is knowledge enough on its own? How does it link with wisdom and insight?

- *"I pray that your hearts will be flooded with light so that you can understand the confident hope he has given..."* Light and understanding go hand in hand. How does God pour his light into our hearts? How does this affect our lives here on earth?

- *"...to those he called – his holy people who are his rich and glorious inheritance."* What does it mean to be called by God? What do you think are the implications?

We all need understanding as we walk with God. Meditating on these amazing prayers will reveal to us God's heart. It helps us to realign our values...

> For me the pull towards work was enticing. We were a company of less than thirty engineers. Every few months, high ranking executives would take the five-hour flight to be wowed by our technology. Car making would never be the same, and the accolades were hard to resist. Yet at home I lived in a ministry house. Together we explored the Bible, and saw many lives changed. God was at work.
>
> Driving between these two worlds it struck me that it was unlikely that there would be cars in heaven. The question was not, "Which world would give me the biggest high?" but "Was I investing my life for eternity?" There was only one answer to that. I wanted my future tied up with God.
>
> I worked with no less commitment on my job. Paul wrote, *"Whatever you do, work at it with all your heart, as working for the Lord, not for human masters"* (Colossians 3:23, NIV). I did the best work I could and gained good results, but there were times when I was asked to make sacrifices, just for appearances, to demonstrate my commitment. This was a road I decided not to go down – and it was noticed.

How are you working with God as he develops you, his inheritance? Read the prayer from Ephesians 1 again. What sacrifices are being asked of you? Pray for God's understanding as you walk in this life. Remember, you are his rich and glorious inheritance.

Eternal Comforter:
BIBLE MEDITATION REVEALS OUR FATHER

We may come to times in our lives when we run out of energy. We get tired of doing good. We need a reason to keep going.

- Think of a time when you felt you should do something, and you were fairly sure it was the right thing to do, but you were tempted to give up. What kept you going?

- In times like those, what did or could have brought encouragement and strength?

Take some time to read this passage from 2 Thessalonians. Pray as you read it.

> Now may our Lord Jesus Christ himself and God our Father, who loved us and by his grace gave us eternal comfort and a wonderful hope, comfort you and strengthen you in every good thing you do and say.
> (2 Thessalonians 2:16-17)

Then add your name in and make it personal. These verses are about your Father in heaven. This is how you might want to start... "Now may my Lord Jesus Christ himself and God my Father, who loves me, (put your name in here), and by his grace gives me eternal comfort…" You might like to write this personal prayer in your diary or journal.

- Often our hearts need encouragement. What is it that encourages you?

- Sometimes we can feel so weak. How do you find strength?

- How have you experienced God in your weakness?

God gives abundantly to those who love him. Paul experienced his strength and comfort. He wanted others to experience it as well. Let's explore these verses some more.

- *"Now may our Lord Jesus Christ himself and God our Father, who loved us…"* What is the defining characteristic of God the Father in this verse?

- *"…and by his grace gave us eternal comfort and a wonderful hope…"* God knows life is hard. Take some time to thank him for his comfort and hope.

- *"…comfort you and strengthen you in every good thing you do and say."* God knows we can lose heart. Pray for him to give you the strength to do what is right. Pray for him to comfort you as you go about your everyday life.

Even though we might not want it to be true, sometimes life will throw us unexpected challenges. I have so often seen God turn it around. He comforts us in unexpected ways…

We looked around our home in dismay. We had rented it out twelve years before, a fully furnished house in good condition. Now we returned to a filthy and trashed shell. Anything that remained had to be thrown into a skip. We prayed to God in distress. What could God say about this destruction of our home? We opened the Bible. *"Shout for joy to the Lord, all the earth."* The text was so incongruous we burst into laughter. What was there that could give us joy?

We were emotionally exhausted after six years overseas. Rebuilding the house would take us a couple of years. Yet these were years of rebuilding our souls, of me being held back from fully re-engaging with ministry for the benefit of my family.

Still the task was too much for us. We prayed for help, and out of the blue a home group from our sending church sent a work party to help us. At a low time in life, God sent his people to comfort and strengthen us. We are forever grateful to God and our friends.

There will be times when you will feel like you are facing something bigger than you can cope with. As we meditate on God's Word, we will begin to relate to our loving Father.

- How do you think God can help you through your present challenges?

- Think back to situations in the past. Can you see how God protected and guided you? It will encourage you for the situations you face today.

- How might you be able to pray in preparation for what is yet to come? God wants to be with you every step of the way.

Unfathomable Fullness:
BIBLE MEDITATION LEADS TO PRAISE

There is a principle that seems to go further than logic: the deeper the hole we find ourselves in, the greater the opportunity to experience the enormity of God's love.

> - Have you ever experienced God rescuing you when it seemed there was no hope? What happened?

> - Have you ever seen God rescue someone you love, and you knew it was a miracle? How did it affect your relationship with God?

Let's make some space to meditate on Scripture in a different way, this time out loud. In Latin, this is called a *Lectio Divina*, a Divine Reading, a time to meet with God.

> - Find a place where you can be out of earshot of others.

> - Ask God to meet with you through the passage in the Bible.

> - Read the passage out loud, so your own ears are hearing the verses read.

> - Pause and reflect on any phrase or statement that stood out to you.

- Read the passage out loud again. Is there a deeper meaning coming to you, particularly from a phrase or statement that first took your attention?

- Reflect on this insight, and then in prayer explain back to God what he has revealed to you.

- Now be silent and listen to God. There might be more he wants to say.

Using Paul's prayer in Ephesians 3, give the *Lectio Divina* a go… You might like to write down your thoughts.

> *I pray that from his glorious, unlimited resources he will empower you with inner strength through his Spirit. Then Christ will make his home in your hearts as you trust in him. Your roots will grow down into God's love and keep you strong. And may you have the power to understand, as all God's people should, how wide, how long, how high, and how deep his love is. May you experience the love of Christ, though it is too great to understand fully. Then you will be made complete with all the fullness of life and power that comes from God.* (Ephesians 3:16-19)

This process will lead us to praise. We will find out that without God it is impossible to live a life pleasing to him. We will experience the fullness of his *"glorious, unlimited resources"*. Yet, it doesn't mean that it will be easy…

Following university, I accepted an engineering job in the USA. For the first few months I felt profound loneliness. I was separated from friends and Christian community. There were many churches full of friendly Christians willing to help, but I could not relate to them. I was going through a spiritual culture-shock, but I made things worse by withdrawing. Soon I found myself unable to pray or read the Bible.

Eventually I realised the only way out was to fight the pain and spend time with God, irrespective of how I felt. Within a month or so of determined feeding on Christ, I began to stabilise. I began to be able to experience Jesus' power in my life. Then I was put in contact with a Navigator group in the city and it felt like coming home. The jigsaw pieces suddenly came together.

Why did I have to go through those months of isolation? The Lord made the purpose clear through Bible meditation and prayer. He was training me to find my strength in him. Only then would I be ready for the great adventure of the next four years.

Whatever your circumstances, it is always possible to look to Jesus. Look again at the verses from Ephesians 3. Let us consider them again.

- Are there situations in your life where you are confronted with your limitations?

- Facing limitations might shake our confidence in God. What does Paul's prayer tell us about how to remain strong in God?

- How can you tap into God's resources? Pray for these verses to impact your life.

Now that you have seen and experienced God, thank him, praise him, adore him, for he is good. He is glorious and unlimited.

TAKING THE LEAP TOWARDS GOD

God calls you on an adventure, and part of that adventure is getting to know him through meditating on his Word. Dare to believe what you are learning. Dare to go on with him. He is worth it.

- He will take you to places that you never dreamed of going. *"Now all glory to God, who is able, through his mighty power at work within us, to accomplish infinitely more than we might ask or think."* (Ephesians 3:20)

- You will experience things that you never dreamed were possible. *"…you will understand the incredible greatness of God's power for us who believe in him."* (Ephesians 1:19)

- You can take the leap into living with God. He accepts you as his own. *"…you will be honored along with him. This is all made possible because of the grace of our God and Lord, Jesus Christ."* (2 Thessalonians 1:12)

Take the leap and get to know God.

ABOUT THE AUTHOR

Derek Leaf is a man with one great passion
– God. He devotes much time to prayer and
Bible meditation, yet it wasn't always that way.
He grew up in an unchurched family, but one
day he picked up a gospel booklet while in
secondary school and came to faith. He didn't
grow much as a Christian until he went to
university and met the Navigators. There he
learned how to meditate on Bible passages and
to meet with God. Derek is married and leads
Navigators UK.

OTHER RESOURCES BY NAVIGATORS UK

All available to buy online at www.navigators.co.uk/online-shop

SEX.LIFE

Ever struggled to open a conversation about sexuality with someone you are discipling? Ever had difficulty navigating a group study on love and relationships? Designed to facilitate honest and open discussion, each of these seven studies begins with a true and raw life story, and features Bible passages, discussion questions and further reflections. This resource equips you to take your group – whatever their beliefs or relationship status – deep into Scripture and their own experiences, empowering them to respond by making changes to their actions and thinking.

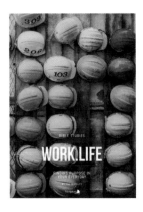

WORK.LIFE

This series of eight studies will empower those you disciple to think well, work well and rest well as they put faith to work. The questions for private study and group discussion are rooted both in the Bible and the everyday realities of work, encouraging real change. The studies are punctuated by quotes from people seeking to integrate their faith and work, pointers to supplementary video content, and homework tasks to help people engage with the topic throughout the week.

PASS THE BATON

Passing on all that Jesus has built into your life is not an easy task. Where do you start, what do you share and with whom? This short book will give you a clear vision for the need to model discipleship 'life on life' in order to make disciples who will make disciples. Using the analogy of a relay race, you'll find it full of clear and practical steps on how to run alongside others to pass on what God has given you, and in such a way that will help them pass it on to others. Those already active in ministry will find this resource both clarifies your vision and grounds your practice of relational and generational disciple making. You will also find it a useful resource to pass on as you seek to envision others in this important ministry.

TIME OUT WITH GOD

How do you relate with a God you cannot see? This short, punchy booklet gives you simple, clear steps on how to take time each day to grow in your relationship with God. Discover the difference even a regular 9-minute slot of prayer, reading the Bible and writing a journal can make to your life. A great resource if you are looking to start this vital habit or to pass on to others if you are involved in disciple making.